"Absolutely and overwhelm... ...g. ...t ...s not a book that can be read in just an hour. The amazing power of pondering the words of each poor man's proverb, quietly forces self-reflection and insight while drawing you closer to a life God intended."

Stacey R. Walters
N.C. Estate Planning Attorney

"What a great read! *Note 2 Self: Faithful Inspiration and Aspiration* provides thought-provoking, insightful and spiritual wisdom to help believers and non-believers overcome life's trials, challenges, and stressors. It also points to the relevance and power of God in today's society. Be prepared to be encouraged, inspired and utilize this practical guide to live an uncompromised life in today's turbulent world. This book paves the way to living a life of excellence in one's career, marriage, family and one's walk with God."

Dr. Anthony C. Hill
Associate Professor of Social Work

"This book makes you think about the value of life!"

Rev. Amos L. Bailey, Sr. Pastor
Christian Faith Baptist Church
Springfield, MA

"This easy read book is filled with pithy sayings that can alter your current behavior. God has enabled Daniel to be very transparent about "truths" that helped transform his life. If applied, they will also impact our lives."

Darryl E. McConnell, Th.B., M. Min., Ph.D.
Faith Baptist Church
Gibsonville, NC

NOTE 2 SELF

FAITHFUL INSPIRATION AND ASPIRATION

DANIEL D. TALLEY

ISBN 978-1-64349-870-6 (paperback)
ISBN 978-1-64349-871-3 (digital)

Christian Faith Publishing, Inc.
832 Park Avenue
Meadville, PA 16335
www.christianfaithpublishing.com

Printed in the United States of America

CONTENTS

INTRODUCTION

Since 2009, God has been ministering to my spirit while giving me little sayings to which I affectionately call *poor man's proverbs*. As God gave them to me, I felt compelled to share them on social media. Oftentimes He would share this information with me while at work. More than a few times, I would be in the midst of performing my job as a cleaning person when He would reveal his thoughts. So off would come gloves and I would begin loading them on social media. It is interesting to note that if I didn't load the sayings on social media right away, I would not remember them.

As time went on, God was urging me to write a book on what He had been giving me. And like some Christian folks, I kept putting it off. Now God knows how hard-headed I am. When He tells me to do something, He usually sends confirmation. In this case, He sent many people to me. Oftentimes people would say "Thank you. Your posts were just what I needed to hear." Now, truthfully, some of the posts were most definitely for me while other people seem to have been the target. If I am being honest, I feel truly blessed that God chose me to be his vessel to deliver this book.

The point of this book is quite simple. It is meant to encourage its readers while inspiring and aspiring them to develop a better relationship with God. We are all at different levels in our relationship with Him. The contents are meant to help us think about our relationship with Him and hopefully, spark a conversation within ourselves as to how we can improve upon that relationship. If the reader does not know Jesus Christ as their Lord and Savior, it is my prayer that this book will help them to seek salvation.

I added some personal life experiences to enhance the enjoyment of the book. You will find some sections to be rather thought-provoking and may cause you to want to make notes to self. It is intended to be used as a personal workbook. Feel free to take full advantage of the *Notes 2 Self* sections found at the bottom of the page. It's your book; take as many notes as you like.

Any profits from the sale of this book will be donated to charity. Enjoy!

Blessings to you all,

Daniel
The Note 2 Self Guy

CHAPTER 1

INSPIRATION

Fuel your anger with pleasantry of thought and your anger becomes a nonfactor.

Listen to a person for twenty minutes with an attentive ear, and the essence of their true character usually presents itself.

At the end of your days, the life you lived will speak for itself.

Remember, God is always there for you to talk to.

Your faith should always be the 800-lb. gorilla in the room.

Notes 2 Self:

_____

_____

_____

_____

_____

_____

_____

Is your faith your calling card?

Love is an action word; Jesus demonstrated it best.

Live to be a blessing to others, and the blessings you give become part of a boomerang phenomenon.

When you help others, the world becomes a better place.

It's okay to be a yes-man as long as the man you are saying yes to is Jesus.

Notes 2 Self:

_____
_____
_____
_____
_____
_____
_____
_____
_____

God has a lot invested in you and is expecting a return on His investment by way of your service.

When you accept Jesus as your Lord and Savior, the nails in your coffin disappear.

The devil considers you a lost cause, while God considers you a worthy cause.

Don't let the devil sucker punch you by offering sinful pleasures presented as godly treats.

Notes 2 Self:

_____

_____

_____

_____

_____

_____

_____

_____

_____

This game called life sure is tricky. Note 2 self: See manual for living—the Bible.

Sometimes waiting for wax to dry on floors takes the patience of Job. There is a lesson in there for you. Oftentimes God provides lessons for us in our daily work.

The act of forgiveness starts with you.

The devil doesn't fight fair; use *the hammer* (the Bible) when fighting against him.

It's okay to spoil God with your praise.

Notes 2 Self:

_____

_____

_____

_____

_____

_____

_____

_____

_____

Spiritual food isn't just for Sundays, you know. Note 2 self: Your soul needs it daily.

Just so you know, the Holy Spirit is an inside job.

A man of integrity will always be appreciated even if he is on the endangered species list.

Try praising God during the bad times and the times won't be bad for long.

Your problems are truly not your own. As God is with you, He shares those problems, too. Note 2 self: Therefore, we should step back and let Him do His *thang*. Sounds simple enough.

Notes 2 Self:

_____

_____

_____

_____

_____

_____

_____

_____

_____

_____

Having a rough day today? Remember who's in control. Chin up my brothers/sisters, God's not worried, and neither should you.

God is not only inside your mind but is the very fabric of your being.

Some people never get a last chance; better get it right—*now!*

Be the man or woman God wants you to be, and the legacy of your life will be fulfilled.

The measure of a man's heart yields great value to those who depend on him.

Notes 2 Self:

_____

_____

_____

_____

_____

_____

_____

_____

_____

Elevation cannot be built on negativity.

It's your life, whatcha gonna do with it?

The Holy Spirit is extraordinarily sensitive to sin, so when it warns you of a pending circumstance or situation—*listen!*

Your approach to a toxic situation makes all the difference in the world.

Don't let your know-it-all spirit get your butt in trouble.

Notes 2 Self:

_____

_____

_____

_____

_____

_____

_____

_____

_____

Will heaven be your reality?

If your faith was the material used to build you a place of dwelling, after construction, would you have a mansion, a nice house by the lake, a shack, or would you be homeless? Note 2 self: Our faith has more power than we realize.

Perfection is an illusion of the mind, while the pursuit of perfection can be a reality. Note 2 self: The Holy Spirit is your coach.

Go out and claim your victory today!

It has been said that a *mind is a terrible thing to waste*, but to waste a soul breaks the Lord's heart.

For some, their lives are ticking time bombs. Let Jesus defuse the bomb.

Notes 2 Self:

_____

_____

_____

_____

_____

_____

_____

_____

Prayer is the building blocks to your faith. Note 2 self: How many blocks have you got?

Has Jesus been calling you? Have you had your calls forwarded? He gives us all many chances to accept him but, eventually, the calls stop (death).

God expects us to be men and women of our word. Remember the promises you made to him.

Invest in the Lord and you will become the darling of the spiritual world.

When you know the word of God, life takes on a different meaning. You see things for what they are, and you are better equipped to handle them. Considering we are living in a world of land mines set by the devil, this is truly a good thing.

Notes 2 Self:

_____

_____

_____

_____

_____

_____

_____

_____

Prayer is more than a ritual. It's actual communication between you and God. And that, my friend, is truly extraordinary.

Don't let the devil hack into your life.

Jesus has more than just a crush on you, He's madly in love with you. He has already given His life for you—proof positive.

A sincere heart goes a long way with He who created everything.

A mental prayer is just as good as a verbal one—both go straight to God's ear.

Notes 2 Self:

_____
_____
_____
_____
_____
_____
_____
_____
_____
_____

CHAPTER 2

GIVE IT SOME THOUGHT

Anger is dynamite with a short lit fuse. Calmness is the water that puts out the fuse.

If you feel your anger must be the 800-lb. gorilla in the room—*leave the room!* Note 2 self: Gotta go!

Alibis won't work with God.

Better own up to the life you are living because, ultimately, God will expect you to.

Some of us will have more to answer for than others. Therefore, just be concerned with one's self.

Notes 2 Self:

_____

_____

_____

_____

_____

_____

_____

_____

The devil has waged war against mankind. Didn't you know? Just watch the news. Note 2 self: Now might be a really good time to review that survival manual (the Bible).

Most people would agree that God can do anything but fail. So when you pray to God to resolve your problem or situation, apply that same logic. Note 2 self: This is more than logic, it is reality.

Many things that have become socially acceptable breaks the heart of God.

What you do is important, but your motives behind your action is equally important. From God's perspective, many a good deed is nullified when the motive is sinful. It's like giving a hungry man a plate of food laced with poison.

Notes 2 Self:

_____

_____

_____

_____

_____

_____

_____

_____

_____

There's not much difference between a bigmouthed Christian and a bigmouthed heathen. Note 2 self: They both need to shut up!

It's a winning proposition—your acceptance of Jesus as Lord and Savior. Note 2 self: The devil knows it, that's why is he's player hatin' (trying to stop your acceptance with sinful delights).

At some point, God is going to get tired of all the shenanigans taking place on planet Earth.

Do ya really want to be known as an average Christian in the halls of heaven or do ya want the angels to say "There goes a primetime player (exceptional Christian) right there" as you walk by? Note 2 self: What you do on this earth will determine that.

Notes 2 Self:

_____

_____

_____

_____

_____

_____

_____

_____

_____

Once the devil has your soul, he considers you yesterday's old news.

When referring to God, influential French scholar Pierre-Simon Laplace once said, "I have no need for that hypothesis." Note 2 self: Laplace died in 1827. I'm thinking Laplace wished he would have had a need for that hypothesis. You don't have to be an intellectual scholar to accept Jesus as your Lord and Savior but rather a willing heart.

Your opinion matters until it violates what thus said the Lord.

The games that people play and yet folks forget that life itself is a game whereby the Righteous Judge evaluates our performance.

The speed of light: 186,000 miles per second. The speed of prayer: instantaneous. Note 2 self: I'm thinking God designed it that way.

Notes 2 Self:

_____

_____

_____

_____

_____

_____

_____

If the devil is the captain of your ship, be prepared to go down with the ship.

Yeah, I know we're not perfect, but many of us can do a whole lot better than what we're doing. Note 2 self: Hmm, I receive.

God cannot bless a sinful situation. Note 2 self: Please stop, as God won't violate His word even for those whom He loves.

For some, you may be the last resort. Note 2 self: Don't give up because you got people counting on you. You can do it!

Both heaven and hell have no occupancy limits. Note 2 self: However, one has a seven-star rating and the other a rating of horror.

Notes 2 Self:

_____

_____

_____

_____

_____

_____

_____

_____

Everything in life has a beginning and ending date. But consider this, everything in the hereafter has only a beginning date. Both heaven and hell have no end date. Note 2 self: The decision is yours. Choose wisely, my friends.

Some day you will see His face (Jesus) whether heaven or hell bound. Note 2 self: The question is—will your meeting be brief or last all of eternity?

Notes 2 Self:

_____

_____

_____

_____

_____

_____

_____

_____

_____

_____

Stay consistently focused on God and the world will appear as it is—a foreign land with a built-in GPS for you to find your way.

Stay focused on God and you develop tunnel vision to the problems of this world.

While at your funeral and people are referring to you, will it be said that the world's loss is heaven's gain?

Notes 2 Self:

_____

_____

_____

_____

_____

_____

_____

_____

_____

Do you want to be known as a man of faith or a man of wealth? Note 2 self: When you pursue one, you sometimes receive the other. I am speaking of faith. Pursuing wealth is usually at the expense of one's faith. The paper chase (money) has a way of becoming the dominant force in one's life and that, my friend, is extraordinarily dangerous.

If you do not consider the devil the enemy, then perhaps it's because you're part of his posse.

In the grand scheme of things, mankind is but a speck in the vast universe, and yet our importance to God is extraordinarily high. Note 2 self: Do you know of any other creation that He sacrificed his Son for? Pretty amazing when you think about it.

Notes 2 Self:

_____
_____
_____
_____
_____
_____
_____
_____
_____
_____

A wise man knows his boundaries yet still strives for greater heights. Note 2 self: Are you such a wise man?

At the end of the day, some things are just *not* worth the price of admission. *Hell* is one of them. What's the price of admission? Your soul.

The devil already knows you're guilty of sinful pleasures. He's offering you an overabundance of them. Note 2 self: Some things just *should not* be on your menu. A strict diet of the fruits of the Spirit should do the trick.

Notes 2 Self:

_____

_____

_____

_____

_____

_____

_____

_____

_____

Nice try Big Bang Theory but God is the architect.

CHAPTER 3

THINGS WE
SHOULD KNOW

Are you a closet Christian? You know, the kind that only comes out when other Christians are around? Note 2 self: God considers closet Christians lukewarm—not a good thing for the closet Christian.

This world is truly on its last leg. Just watch the news.

The power of prayer is greater than any weapon aimed at you. Prayers are whispers in the ears of God from those whom He loves. And when the prayers are built upon faith, the whispers become mental images in the mind of God. Note 2 self: You best believe He hears you.

For the fellas, God will hold you accountable as the head of your household. Don't hide behind your queen. Brother man, it's your responsibility.

Notes 2 Self:

_____

_____

_____

For fathers with a daughter(s): If your baby girl(s) grew up to marry a man just like you, would you be pleased? Believe it or not, your example is setting the stage.

Man or woman of God: Be mindful of the music, books, magazines, and movies that you entertain. Has the Holy Spirit given them the GA designation? By the way, GA stands for God Approved.

For the ladies: If he is morally bankrupt, don't waste your time with him. If he is truly a man who loves the Lord, opportunity may await you. God loves you. He wouldn't send you garbage.

I believe hell has executive suites reserved for those who willfully do the devil's bidding. Note 2 self: The torment and pain experienced in the executive suites far exceed those in other areas of hell. Oh, let me guess, the devil failed to mention this minor detail. Reserve your ticket to heaven. See Jesus for details.

Notes 2 Self:

_____

_____

_____

_____

_____

_____

_____

In the end times, the Antichrist will gather a 200-million-man army to fight Jesus (Revelation 9:16). Note 2 the Antichrist: Really, dude, can a man fight God? I'm thinking *no!*

The enemy (Jesus) of your enemy (the devil) is not only your friend but is also your Savior.

Whatever happens, conduct yourselves in a manner worthy of the gospel of Christ (Philippians 1:27). It is your duty and responsibility.

Prayer does more than change things, it takes root to one's mind-set and begins to eliminate the problem before it develops. Note 2 self: Next to calling on the name of Jesus, it's probably the most effective weapon against the devil and his henchmen.

Take a good look at the character of your friends, and your character becomes apparent to the observer. Birds of a feather do what? I think you know the answer. Note 2 self: Be careful who you surround yourself with.

Notes 2 Self:

_____

_____

_____

_____

_____

_____

The thing about temptation is that God always gives us a way out. Look for the exit sign in neon lights. Note 2 self: The illuminated exit sign is always there; it's just that our desire to sin causes us to wear very dark sunglasses, thus minimizing the illumination of the exit sign. Take off the shades and run for the exit sign.

Thank God that He doesn't view mankind by the sum total of our actions, but mainly by the action of one—acceptance of His Son Jesus as Lord and Savior.

Make your faith your life jacket. Note 2 self: It will sustain you through all of life's trials and tribulations.

Straightjacket sin because if you don't, it will straight-jacket you.

Keep your eye on the prize—pleasing God.

Notes 2 Self:

_____

_____

_____

_____

_____

_____

_____

_____

_____

CHAPTER 4

ON THE LIGHTER SIDE

Can ya really get pissed off if you buy something from the dollar store and it doesn't work as advertised? Probably not.

Ever had a person take off their shoes and immediately the area smells like corn chips? Similarly, but in a good way, when you open your mouth your words should be filled with goodness. Note 2 self: Your words are to be a blessing to others.

"I may be crazy but I *ain't* stupid," said the chicken who was invited to a KFC convention. Note 2 self: Every open invitation is not for you, so be selective.

The devil got some folks in a straightjacket and, sadly, they're okay with it.

Notes 2 Self:

_____

_____

_____

_____

_____

One day my sixteen-year-old son said to me, "Dad, one day I will make you proud of me." I quietly said to myself, "That's what I want to hear." But then, his next words were, "But that might take a while." I responded, "So will I be alive to see?" To which he responded, "I'm not sure…"

One day, I took my son and my daughter to the soup kitchen to help pass out food to the less fortunate. This was to be a teachable moment as, by the grace of God, we are blessed with food to eat. I was so proud of them. They eagerly and joyfully helped the soup kitchen staff with whatever was asked of them in serving. Upon leaving, we get into the car and both of these knuckleheads asked in unison, "So how much do we get for this?" Lord, where have I gone wrong?

So I asked my teenage son what his plans were for the future. He told me that plan A was for him to attend college, study video game design, and become a professional tennis player. Plan B was to live with a friend and get a job at McDonald's. Note 2 self: Call me crazy but I'll be rooting for plan A. Plan B is a serious drop off from plan A, but at least the kid's got a backup plan.

Notes 2 Self:

_____

_____

_____

_____

_____

Oftentimes our greatest enemy is our willingness to listen to the devil. Invest in a good pair of earplugs, if you must.

When Jesus looks over your life, will He be smiling or frowning?

Ever heard of birds chirping (singing) early in the a.m.? Kinda sounds like they are praising God. Note 2 self: Man, you gonna let the little birdies outdo ya?

You might be a lukewarm Christian if you only go to church on Sunday and people only know that you're a Christian by the *badge* that you wear.

Much of the future depends on your non-activation of bonehead decisions.

Notes 2 Self:

_____
_____
_____
_____
_____
_____
_____
_____
_____

One day in church the choir was singing, and I begin to sing along with them. At the end of the song, a lady sitting one row ahead of me turned around and said, "Young man, you have a beautiful voice." My daughter, who was sitting next to me, turned to me and said, "Obviously, that woman is deaf because she doesn't know what she is talking about!"

He doesn't love you, he just wants to mess you around. It's a perpetual game of cat and mouse, and I'll give you one guess who's the mouse. Note 2 self: This *ain't* an episode of Tom and Jerry, the devil is playing for keeps!

I said it once and I'll say it again. Hell is filled with players and playettes, while heaven is filled with former players and playettes who love the Lord. Note 2 self: For all, change must take place.

When you stand up for Jesus, you're gonna piss some folks off—namely, the devil and his hired hands.

Notes 2 Self:

_____

_____

_____

_____

_____

_____

_____

The sky is His canvas - awesome!

CHAPTER 5

SAY IT AIN'T SO

What's your soul worth? Apparently, quite a bit. Why else would the devil attempt to acquire it by any means necessary?

The devil doesn't always show up as a wolf in sheep's clothing. Sometimes he shows up as friends or family. Note 2 self: Sad but unfortunately true.

Just in case you were wondering, God sees your inappropriate emails, text messages, and pictures.

Hell is a one-way ticket. Note 2 self: Something the devil doesn't want mankind to know.

On Judgment Day, many of us will be in the negotiating mood. Note 2 self: God will not be.

Notes 2 Self:

_____

_____

_____

_____

_____

Hell has no early release programs. Once you're in, you're in.

Sometimes the wolf in sheep's clothing is a fake Christian.

Eight ball in the corner packet—that's what the devil is trying to do to mankind.

Imagine a world without hope…Don't look now, but you are at the gates of hell.

The devil is the father of all lies and half-truths. He can promise and give you the whole world, but in the end, death and destruction will be your eternal bedfellows.

Notes 2 Self:

_____

_____

_____

_____

_____

_____

_____

_____

_____

Remember, you are what you are because you chose to be.

Life is not a game. Your eternity is at stake. And the devil is playing for keeps.

Whether you believe or not, you will someday meet Jesus face-to-face. What are you going to say?

The life we live is either an investment in heaven or hell. Note 2 self: We are, in effect, saving for our eternal future.

Notes 2 Self:

_____
_____
_____
_____
_____
_____
_____
_____
_____

You can roll the dice with the devil or opt for the sure thing with Jesus. Note 2 the gambler: The choice is yours.

Sometimes the blessings of God have a delayed effect. But, remember, the greater blessing is in His timing. Note 2 self: This will only make sense when you have experienced it.

The day the man in the mirror looks like someone else will be the day you can blame someone else for your mistakes.

Good or bad—you will be an example for someone today.

Notes 2 Self:

_____

_____

_____

_____

_____

_____

_____

_____

_____

_____

You drop an f-bomb on the devil every time you pray to God. Note 2 self: Bombs away...

You are running a race against time. Wasted time is an ally of the devil. Accomplish your mission in life while praising and thanking God for giving you the resources to do so.

Do you really want to spend eternity wishing you had accepted Jesus as Lord and Savior? Note 2 self: Probably the prevailing thought of those in hell.

Is God bragging on you to his angels or is he in silent mode?

Notes 2 Self:

_____

_____

_____

_____

_____

_____

_____

_____

_____

_____

Rainbows by land or sea - God is amazing!

CHAPTER 6

SIMPLISTIC LOGIC

When sin is all around you, just get up and leave.

"The logic of mankind is fundamentally flawed,"—something Jesus might say.

What you entertain in your mind is reflected in your actions.

I have learned that we can honor God in many ways, but to honor Him in our thoughts is probably the most important. Why is that, you ask? Think about it. From thought comes all actions. You honor Him in thought, and honorable actions are sure to follow.

If you were to calculate the square root of love, you would find the heart of God.

Notes 2 Self:

_____

_____

_____

_____

_____

Heaven is not automatic without the acceptance of Jesus as Lord and Savior. Hell, on the other hand, certainly is.

Each day thousands die and go to heaven or hell. Note 2 self: When your time comes, do ya know where you're headed?

Sometimes lightning strikes twice simply because we keep doing the same stupid stuff. Note 2 self: Enough already—just stop!

Your children need your love and support like the air you breathe.

Notes 2 Self:

_____

_____

_____

_____

_____

_____

_____

_____

_____

Love may not begin with forgiveness but it certainly cannot grow without it.

Grab opportunity today and show it what you are made of.

Shut the devil up. Start praying.

To God, our lives are an open book.

God's blessings come with a posse of life-changing events.

Notes 2 Self:

_____

_____

_____

_____

_____

_____

_____

_____

_____

Focusing on God tends to shrink problems to undetectable levels.

A blessing is no one-time event; it has friends.

Helping others is investing in the kingdom of God. Note 2 self: I understand God keeps excellent records.

Jesus loves you from so many angles. His love transcends space and time yet is ever-present.

Notes 2 Self:

_____

_____

_____

_____

_____

_____

_____

_____

_____

CHAPTER 7

IT'S A FAIR QUESTION

If birds of a feather flock together, then who are you flocking with? Note 2 self: A question worthy of consideration. Consider the qualities of your flocking buddy.

The life you live is a work of art. At the end of life, either it's worthy to be put in a museum or a thrift shop.

The devil considers a proactive Christian a menace to society. Note 2 the Christian: So the question in the devil's mind is—are you a menace to society or does he consider you a nonthreat?

We are always telling God what we need, but how often do we ask God what he needs from us?

Is your brand of Christianity giving Jesus a black eye?

Are you cashing checks your soul won't be able to cash?

Notes 2 Self:

_____

_____

_____

_____

_____

_____

One thing God will never say to mankind—what secrets are you hiding from me?

God is looking for a few good men (women included), are you interested?

Are you a praying machine?

Every time you tell someone that you're a Christian, is the devil somewhere laughing his head off?

Is your belief in God your claim to fame? Note 2 self: The devil is hoping not.

The life you have is on loan from God. Are you using the time wisely?

Notes 2 Self:

_____

_____

_____

_____

_____

_____

_____

_____

_____

_____

Is God your addiction?

Do you really trust God? That is the fundamental question of your faith.

Are you starving yourself spiritually?

Is God your power source or is it your bank account?

Note 2 men: If you're an example of what a man should be, do we need another example?

God is a jealous God and rightfully so. Have you given Him a reason to be jealous?

If Jesus is your partner, why are you dancing with the devil?

Notes 2 Self:

_____
_____
_____
_____
_____
_____
_____
_____
_____

What if heaven is far better than described, and hell is far worse? Note 2 self: Would that alter how we live our lives?

Is the devil using you for target practice? Arm yourself with the Word and fight back!

If people could see your inner you when approaching you, would they cross the street or greet you with a smile? Note 2 self: At the end of the day, is it that inner you that they will remember?

If your doubt was a person, would it be big man on campus or some dude rarely seen by others? Note 2 self: Both God and the devil are interested in your answer.

On that great day of reckoning, will you be placed on the right or the left of Jesus? Note 2 self: The condition of your eternity depends upon it.

Notes 2 Self:

_____

_____

_____

_____

_____

_____

_____

_____

Do you love God because of who He is or because of what He can do for you?

Are you spiritually fit?

Is God your ace boon coon (best friend)?

Time isn't unlimited, so why do many approach it as if it is?

Does your execution of Christianity make God sick to his stomach?

Know your reality. Heaven bound or that other place?

Team Jesus or not? Pretty simple question, but the answer means everything as we know it and beyond.

Psst... Jesus can save you. Pass the word.

Notes 2 Self:

_____

_____

_____

_____

_____

_____

_____

CHAPTER 8

Just Plain Good Advice

Your best plan is not even on God's radar, but because He's God, He still knows about it. Note 2 self: Psst... He's got a better plan for ya!

Call me stupid but one who is thankful gives God incentive to want to do more. Note 2 self: Ungratefulness is a blessing assassin.

Even in the midst of chaos, God provides a blessing. Note 2 self: Just know that it's there and search for it.

How you live your life is your most effective witnessing tool.

At the end of the day, some things are just *not* worth the price of admission. Your soul.

Notes 2 Self:

_____

_____

_____

_____

_____

_____

Being a blessing to others is your duty as a follower of the King. Others see Him through your kindness and way of life. Note 2 self: Not only is it your duty but also your responsibility.

Are you a court jester for the devil? Note 2 self: If Jesus is absent from your life, then the answer is a resounding *yes*.

A thousand excuses—all without merit. And then comes the judgment.

No mystery for the Christian—God lives in you. Note 2 self: The question is—have you given Him the basement apartment or the penthouse suite?

Notes 2 Self:

_____

_____

_____

_____

_____

_____

_____

_____

_____

Love God with an unbridled heart.

When we fear God, we begin to learn of our place in the universe.

God's got you covered.

In the eyes of man, justice may not be swift, but on God's timetable, it is most assuredly certain. Note 2 self: Don't worry about the misdeeds of others but rather focus on your own.

Notes 2 Self:

_____

_____

_____

_____

_____

_____

_____

_____

_____

_____

CHAPTER 9

NOTE 2 THE CHRISTIAN

God has a plan for you, and so does the devil. Note 2 self: Remember Jeremiah 29:11.

Pretend Jesus is standing right next to you and He is shadowing you for the day. Would your conversations with people change? What about the text messages or emails that you send? Any change in your actions? What about your thoughts or motives? You don't have to pretend—He's there. Now does that change anything?

The devil may say to you "Your wish is my command." Be advised, it's always at a cost. So beware.

Your faith in Christ Jesus is your safe house and the devil knows it. Why else would he have demons of doubt assigned to you?

Notes 2 Self:

_____

_____

_____

_____

_____

_____

Feeling a little down on yourself? Consider what God said of man in Psalms 8:5, "You made Him a little lower than the heavenly beings and crowned Him with glory and honor." Seems to me, God deems you pretty important.

How can you have a testimonial without the test? Get ready for the test.

Review God's escape plan—John 3:16.

When you read the Bible, pay close attention to the words written in red as that is Jesus Himself speaking directly. Talk about getting it straight from the horse's mouth. Much of what He says leaves no wiggle room (room for interpretation). It is what it is. God has spoken, but are you listening?

God expects us to be men and women of our word. Remember the promises you made to Him.

Notes 2 Self:

_____

_____

_____

_____

_____

_____

_____

_____

From your lips directly to God's ear are the prayers of the righteous. Gotta love it!

When you are angry with God because He's not explaining to you why you are having to endure a situation or circumstance, read Job 38 and assume God is talking directly to you. Note 2 self: Stops me in my tracks every time.

When you know the word of God, life takes on a different meaning. You see things for what they are, and you are better equipped to handle them. Considering we are living in a world of land mines set by the devil, this is truly a good thing.

When you make the best of a bad situation, God illuminates the exit route.

You've got a cheering section in heaven. Ask the Holy Spirit to let you hear the cheers.

Notes 2 Self:

_____

_____

_____

_____

_____

_____

_____

The devil's motto: Live a life for me or live a life for yourself at the exclusion of God. Either way, at the end of life, your soul will belong to the devil. Note 2 self: Don't fall for the trap!

Fact or fiction: Lord, I am living my life to please you. Note 2 self: Only you and God truly know the answer.

If you were the last Christian left on earth, could you carry the torch, or would Christianity die with you?

Notes 2 Self:

_____

_____

_____

_____

_____

_____

_____

_____

_____

_____

CHAPTER 10

GOT A WORD FOR YA!

Do not be misled. "Bad company corrupts good character" (1 Corinthians 15:33). Note 2 self: No room for interpretation here. Hang around people and we are influenced by them. Hang around a dude who curses all the time and eventually you will be the owner of more than a few *four*-letter words. If we keep good company, I bet the reverse is true as well. Watch the company you keep, homey!

Do you want to have *peace* in your life? You do? *Great!* Philippians 4:8–9 gives us the recipe for peace. "Finally, brothers, whatever is true, whatever is noble, whatever is right, whatever is pure, whatever is lovely, whatever is admirable – if any is excellent or praiseworthy—think about such things. Whatever you have learned or received or heard from me or seen in me—put it into practice. And the God of peace will be with you." Note 2 self: This is our road map to peace. Let's caravan together as we embark upon this wonderful journey. Remember to keep our minds focused on God; it is the most direct route to peace. We can do it!

When we learn to tithe instead of tipping God, we unlock the door containing financial abundance. Note 2

self: Tithing is a growing process but do yourself a favor—
Grow up *fast* as you may be leaving blessings on the table.
Study Malachi 3:6–11.

Notes 2 Self:

_____

_____

_____

_____

_____

_____

_____

_____

_____

Sometimes we should just *shut up* and *stop whining!* What do you mean, homey? Philippians 2:14–15 gives us some very helpful advice: "Do everything without finding fault or arguing. Then you will be pure and without blame. You will be children of God without fault in a sinful and evil world. Among the people of the world you shine like stars in the heavens." Note 2 self: Folks who continue on without whining demonstrate a sense of silent strength and perseverance that is admired by man and God. Silence can be golden!

Want to hear some *good news,* homey? First Corinthians 2:9 should have those of us who truly love God jumping out of our skin with excitement! It reads, "However, as it is written: 'No eye has seen, no ear has heard, no mind has conceived' what God has prepared for those who love Him." Beloved children of God, close your eyes and imagine all the gifts you are to receive, and the reality is—we're not even close! Note 2 non-lovers/non-followers of God: This scripture probably means nothing to you. But my brothers and sisters, it really should because at the end of the day your loss will be exponentially great!

Notes 2 Self:

_____

_____

_____

_____

_____

_____

If you were in the devil's court, would there be enough evidence to convict you of being a Christian? If the evidence is overwhelming, God is pleased. However, if you are convicted due to circumstantial evidence, I would be very concerned. Why? Revelation 3:16 provides some insight: "So because you are lukewarm—neither hot nor cold—I am about to spit you out of my mouth." God *does not* approve of lukewarm Christians; they are considered vomit. Note 2 self: Being a borderline Christian (lukewarm Christian) is not a good position to be in. Don't have one foot in the world and the other in the Word. That is a dangerous existence, my friend!

The 23rd Psalm starts off with "The Lord is my shepherd, I shall not be in want." Do we not realize what that truly means? A shepherd can be defined as one who leads a flock (in this case, His people) down the right path, cares for them, and protects them from danger. God certainly has the resources as He is the creator of everything and owns it all. You see, sheep aren't very smart animals (humans aren't much smarter when compared to God). Therefore, our shepherd (Lord) will provide all our needs, will care for us, and direct our paths. Note 2 self: Wow! All that and that's just verse 1! Tell me more.

Notes 2 Self:

_____

_____

_____

_____

Unfortunately, there are people out here who ruin their lives with riotous living, and are pissed off with God because they end up with nothing but a misery of regret. You know, God warned us of such in Proverbs 19:3, "A man's own folly ruins his life, yet his heart rages against the Lord." Note 2 self: God didn't do it; we did it to ourselves.

"Avoid every kind of evil," says 1 Thessalonians 5:22. Note 2 self: For many of us, this means a total lifestyle make-over. It means the elimination of friends, relationships, conversations, and questionable situations. Birds of a feather may flock together, but now it's time to leave the flock.

Roman 8:37 says, "No, in all these things we are more than conquerors through Him who loved us." Therefore, let the record show you are more than a conqueror through Christ Jesus! Note 2 self: The devil hopes that you will forget that. Prove him wrong, my brothers and sisters. More than a conqueror means exceeding above your situation. In other words, suppose your situation was debt—you come out of debt and now you are in the position to help others who are in debt by virtue of the resources that God has given you. Yeah, the devil better *step off.*

Notes 2 Self:

_____

_____

_____

_____

Unless you are a minister, a monk, or perhaps a nun, your marital vows (oaths) may be the only vow you ever make to God. *News flash*—God expects us to keep our vows. In Matthew 5:33, Jesus Himself says, "Again, you have heard that it was said to the people long ago, 'Do not break your oath, but keep the oaths you have made to the Lord.'" Note 2 self: If you are married or getting ready to get *hitched*, do everything within your power to make it work because God will ask you, "So how did you do on that promise you made to me?" He will only be interested in your contributions or lack thereof to the marriage. Don't worry, He will ask the same of your spouse. The blame game will not work. Remember, your wedding vows are more than just words.

Does the devil have a nuclear warhead aimed at you? What! You heard me! First Peter 5:8 tells us, "Be alert and of sober mind. Your enemy the devil prowls around like a roaring lion looking for someone to devour." The devil uses sex, drugs, alcohol, greed, lust, porn, worldly living, a lying tongue, and a prideful heart. These are but a few of his weapons, but his nuclear warhead is the destruction of the family. If he can break up the family, then each individual member becomes very susceptible to his attack. Note 2 self: "Therefore, put on the full armor of God, so that when the day of evil comes, you may be able to stand your ground, and after you have done everything, to stand. Stand firm then, with the belt of truth buckled around your waist, with the breastplate of righteousness in place" (Ephesians 6:13–14).

Notes 2 Self:

_____

_____

_____

_____

_____

_____

_____

_____

_____

_____

Hey, fellas, does God love your woman? First Peter 3:7 answers this very question. "Husbands, in the same way be considerate as you live with your wives, and treat them with respect as the weaker partner and as heirs with you of the gracious gift of life, so that nothing will hinder your prayers." God loves and values your woman so much that He is warning you that if you mistreat her, that when you pray to Him, He will be like, "Talk to the hand." Note 2 the fellas: Ever wonder why God seems not to be answering your prayers? You may want to check the way you are treating your wife. So does God love your woman? *He most certainly does!*

Need another reason why we should obey God? Here you go. "Now then, my sons, listen to me; blessed are those who keep my ways" (Proverbs 8:28). Note 2 self: Now God has at least a couple of billion ways He can bless us. The mystery is the nature of the blessing, but the certainty is the blessing itself. Like any good parent, God wants to reward his children for their obedience. So have you been a good child?

So you want God's attention? You want Him to hear your prayers. Well, 1 Peter 3:12 gives us the inside scoop. "For the eyes of the Lord are on the righteous and His ears are attentive to their prayer, but the face of the Lord is against those who do evil." Note 2 self: Did you also catch that thing about "The face of the Lord is against those who do evil?" Stay away from evil, brother man!

Notes 2 Self:

_____

_____

_____

_____

_____

_____

_____

_____

_____

_____

CHAPTER 11

IT'S YOUR TIME

"For God so loved the world that He gave His one and only Son, that whoever believes in Him shall not perish but have eternal life" (John 3:16). In other words, God loved us so much that He sent His only Son on a suicide mission so that we might have an opportunity at eternal life with Him. It is God's will that we all be saved (1 Timothy 2:4), but God is a gentleman. We must come to Him of our own free will.

If you want to be saved, say the next paragraph with a sincere heart and mind and you will be saved.

"Lord, I recognize that I am a sinner and that I need you in my life. I ask for your forgiveness. I believe Jesus died on the cross for my sins so that I can be saved. Lord, I love you and will do my best to live a life that is representative of you and will do my best to adhere to your commands. In Jesus' name, amen!"

Congratulations! This will prove to be the best decision you have ever made.

Notes 2 Self:

Salvation birthday: _____

    If you have said the prayer of salvation as a result of reading this book, make a note 2 self and contact me via email (thenote2selfguy@gmail.com). If you have any questions or comments, feel free to reach out to me. For more information, go to www.note2selfseries.com May God be with you my friends.

—Daniel D. Talley
The Note 2 Self Guy

ABOUT THE AUTHOR

by Conrad Talley
(Brother of Author)

 If God's great aspiration is humanity, one device of His eternal genius, then through men He would yield inspiration—vessels by which His will has been done. Among many throughout our time, there is such a man.

Daniel Denolius Talley was born in Detroit, Michigan, and the eldest son of four children. From humble upbringings, a hard work ethic was demonstratively instilled by his mother, Vinette Talley, concurrently coupled by the disciplinary tutelage of his father, Danny E. Talley. Serious and astute, Danny, as he is affectionately called, excelled scholastically to eventually graduate high school in 1985. He later embarked upon a military career serving in the United States Air Force which would change his life forever.

In October of 1986, while stationed in the United Kingdom, Daniel committed himself to the Christian faith receiving Jesus Christ as his personal Lord and Savior. He heard and responded to God's call—a path that has proceeded to spiritual accomplishment and personal success. In 1990, Daniel returned to the United States and enrolled at Howard University, a prestigious historically black university. There, he studied business management with the objective of climbing the corporate ladder. During this grueling period, Daniel worked two jobs utilizing proceeds from the military which put him through school. He later graduated with honors in 1993 with a bachelor's degree in business administration.

Daniel's post-college transition would lead him down several career paths, traveling from Washington, DC, Pennsylvania, Massachusetts, and finally to North Carolina where he now resides with his loving wife Torriah and two children Da'Ryeus and Wisdom.

The ambitious human resource manager jumpstarted a commercial cleaning business which prosperously took him out of the corporate limelight. Then, suddenly, in the year 2009, Daniel began receiving holy inklings to record phrases of Christian sentiment. These memoirs were later compiled into literature culminating to what readers know as *Note 2 Self: Faithful Inspiration and Aspiration.*

From his mortal genesis to present day, Daniel has achieved every pursuit of interest he sought. His series of five-year plan goals have served him well. Perhaps his most meaningful quest is the contents of this book in the hope of bringing many to Jesus Christ as humanly possible, leaving behind a God-bestowed legacy to encourage, comfort, and inspire.

CPSIA information can be obtained
at www.ICGtesting.com
Printed in the USA
LVHW010422050119
602853LV00014B/30/P